All Kinds of Jokes
for All Kinds of Folks

Copyright © 2019 By Kelly Smith
All Rights Reserved
Printed in the U.S.A. by Kindle Direct Publishing
ISBN 978-0-9820954-4-7

No part of this book may be reproduced or transmitted in any form or by any means, electronic, graphic, optical or mechanical, including photocopying, recording, taping, electronic data, internet packets or by another storage or retrieval method without written permission of the publisher. For information contact KellyStaffingExpert61@gmail.com

The opinions expressed in this book are those of the author. Mention or photos of persons, businesses, institutions does not imply endorsement of this book by mentioned or photographed persons, businesses or institutions.

The information in this book is based on actual situations and documents. The names and other identifying characteristics of the individuals and employers have been changed or removed in order to protect their privacy.

Front and back cover design by John Low and team www.ebooklaunch.com

This book is dedicated to my late cousin, Jenny. Jenny and I would spend hours drinking root beer and telling jokes until we were slaphappy. Well into the morning hours we would tell each other endless one-liners, story jokes and make crank phone calls to unsuspecting grocery clerks and sometimes whomever was on the other line of the random number that we dialed. When Jenny and I got together the world was one big laugh-fest ... that is until we started telling spooky stories, but that can wait for another book.

The following is a culmination of over five decades of material I have amassed through diaries, notes, newspaper articles and memories of telling jokes as a kid. I used to love spending the night at my cousin Jenny's house, which was located out in the country in the farmlands of Michigan. At night you couldn't see your hand in front of you. We would stay up sometimes till two in the morning telling spooky stories, jokes and story jokes or pulling dumb pranks like calling the local country store and asking if they had Prince Albert in a can. They would reply that they did, thinking we would come down and purchase the tobacco but instead we would tell the clerk to "Let him out!" Then we would giggle as we hung up the phone. Later in my life when I was a young woman trying to make it as a stand-up comedienne in Los Angeles I was fortunate enough to attend a couple of private parties at *The Improv* on Melrose Avenue. Owner, Budd Friedman, would advise the comedians that the best thing they could do was to write as many jokes as possible every day. Budd said that for every one hundred jokes we wrote, maybe one would be really funny. I followed Budd's advice and have written countless jokes, stories and funny material of all sorts. I hope that you agree that at least some of the material included in this book will be the truly humorous parts of my decades-long effort to write the funny.

Contents

Being Silly is Funny 1
Work is Funny 7
Men & Women are Funny 13
Offensive Funny Stuff 23
Getting Old is Funny 31
Old Timey Story Jokes are Funny 35
Funny Songs 43
Funny Words & Sayings 57
God, He's Funny! 63

Being Silly is Funny

Q: Why won't cannibals eat comedians?
A: They taste funny

Q: What do you call a cow with no legs?
A: Ground beef

Q: What did the cow name her baby calf?
A: Patty

Q: How much did the cow's baby calf weigh when it was born?
A: A quarter pound

Q: What did one ocean say to the other?
A: Nothing, they just waved

I've got a frog in my throat…tastes like chicken.

We were so poor, the only family pets we had were dust bunnies.

Q: Why don't scientists trust atoms?
A: Because they make up everything

Q: What kind of exercises do lazy people do?
A: Diddly-squats

Q: What kind of socks do Christians wear?
A: Holey ones

Q: Why don't calculus majors throw house parties?
A: Because you should never drink and derive

Q: What does Charles Dickens keep in his spice rack?
A: The best of thymes, the worst of thymes

Q: Have you heard about the new restaurant called Karma?
A: there's no menu; you get what you deserve

Q: What happened when the blonde, brunette and redhead tried to swim across the river?

A: The blonde got tired halfway across and decided to turn back

Q: What did the elephant say to the naked man?
A: How do you breathe with that thing?

Q: What do you have when you have a half a dozen lawyers up to their necks in cement?
A: Not enough cement

Q: What does the rich lady say to her baby?
A: Gucci, Gucci, Gucci

Q: How did Captain Hook die?
A: Jock itch

Q: What did the dinner plate say to the cups?
A: Dinner is on me tonight

Q: What do you call a hot dog without its insides?
A: A hallow-weenie

Q: Why didn't the skeleton go to the dance?
A: He had no body

Q: What did the Mexican fire chief name his twin sons?
A: Hose A and Hose B

Q: What did the seamstress name her twin daughters?
A: Poly and Esther

Q: What brand of ice cream do pigs prefer?
A: Haagen-Dazs

Thank God it's Friday. But don't celebrate with a glass of wine; I hear the wine stompers in Italy are having a sit-in.

They ought to rename Starbucks to Steal-Bucks

I hear Starbucks is starting a new sorority on campuses across the USA it is called, Kappa Kappa Chino. Not to be outdone, Anheuser-Busch is starting a fraternity called, I Tappa Keg.

I work too much. I never have time to date. I'm beginning to think my gravestone will read, "Here lies Kelly; still sleeping alone."

I jay walked across the street and stubbed my toe. I called a toe truck and they were angry that I couldn't foot the bill. This was my third offense so they took my shoes away.

There is a location in Michigan called Mackinac Island where no automobiles are allowed. The main mode of transportation is by horse. The island is famous for its' fudge. If you ask me, there's something odd about an island that is famous for its' fudge where there is an abundance of horses. The last time I was there I could have sworn a horse laughed at me while I was eating a piece of fudge.

Feeling run-down and low on energy I decided to visit our local vitamin store. The salesperson recommended I take bee-pollen tablets to increase my energy. I doubled the dosage. Three days later I feel buzzed, am drawn to lights and keep flinging myself against screen doors.

Work is Funny

I work for a good cause, 'cause I need the money.

Work: the ultimate self-esteem, sucking machine.

I work at an "I'll scratch your back, you stab mine" kind of place.

You know you'll be working more than 40 hours a week at that new job when on your first day of employment they issue you a badge, lap-top, cell phone and sleeping bag.

The other day I heard a commercial where some nincompoop proudly says, "I've got three speeding tickets, two auto accidents, and one DUI. What I need is affordable insurance." I'm thinking, no what you need is to ride the damn bus!

I underestimated how difficult it would be to work till your old. I'm so tired at work. The other day I dropped a paper clip, I bent down to pick it up and thought, "What else can I get while I'm down here?"

Bring your daughter to work day, or as I like to refer to it: Marry rich or this is how you'll end up one day-day.

You know the stress level has gotten out of hand when you find yourself at lunchtime standing in front of the microwave yelling, "HURRY!"

I'm a Recruiter. I recruit I.T. computer professionals. Some of the names of my candidates can be very difficult to pronounce as they come from many different countries. Last week I was working with Mr. Song Shin Shu, or as I like to refer to him, Song Shin Shu (sung to the tune of Song Sung Blue by Neil Diamond) every garden grows one.

Our workplace reminds me of Hell; you're damned if you do and damned if you don't.

Our office fridge doesn't have a crisper, it's more like a rotter.

I don't drink coffee at work, it keeps me awake.

The barista had out three tip jars. The first one read, "Thanks a latte" the second one read, "Feeling Tipsy?" and the third read, "Don't make me put a bug in your drink"

Our new boss is so ugly it is difficult to take her seriously. Even if we squint, she still looks like a Basset Hound in a bonnet.

I work too much. I never have time to date. I'm beginning to think my gravestone will read, "Here lies Kelly; still sleeping alone."

Dogs serving on the police force are great but what I think we need are monkey's on the team. Clip a badge on a monkey and let it loose. It's faster and meaner than a dog could ever be. Sure a bite from a dog is scary but try to hide in a bush or in a tree with a monkey hooting and hollering and swinging from limb-to-limb coming at you full speed. Imagine trying to get a monkey off your back while they are pulling on your ears. All the police officer would have to do is yell, "Don't make me let KoKo go crazy on your bad self!" and the bad person would come running towards you begging for mercy.

During the job interview I told the manager that I could type 100 words a minute. Amazed, they asked me to show them this skill that I possessed. "No problem", I replied. I sauntered over to a nearby table where there was an electric typewriter; I put my index finger on the letter 'I' and held it there.

In addition to writing jokes and performing comedy I work as a corporate recruiter.

Over the years I have received some pretty interesting resumes, emails and cover letters. Following are a few of my favorites.

Good Morning Ms. Smith: During my 1.5 hour drive home yesterday, I replayed our earlier conversation....every pause, hesitancy and voice quiver. Needless to say, I wanted a 'do over'...of course, we don't get second chances to make first impressions BUT there are two items I wanted to address:

1) SQL - during the data conversion for Ford's GOLDD project, I supervised the programmer writing

---

Josh 2 A2.doc

Dear Sir or Madam,

I was very titillated to see your advertisement for a File Retention Coordinator in the Ann Arbor News. I have been seeking such an opportuni as this, and I think my background and your requirements may be a good match. I am diligent, personable, and analytical. I earned a Bachelor o Business Administration degree, with a major concentration in Computer Information Systems, from Eastern Michigan University.

I look forward to hearing from you! My resume is enclosed as an attachme

---

Cover Letter:
Job Number 99999
Event Number 2352

I am a student who is kind of confused on what my job title is. And I am looking for a little assistance from this company to assist me in choosing a good field and knowing about other fields that are related to what I want to do in life. First im going to tell you what I like to do, and what I want to do, I like to do things on the computer and I really would like to become a computer designer who designs things on the computer or making a program or testing something. All I know is that I would like a very good job with a high salary. If you could send me some information on all the jobs dealing with what I like, and how much they make and what they do and what is the most highest paying job for computers. I am a very determined student and will do anything to be very succesful, but I just need a little assistance and a little information on it. I am very intersted in being in

ALL KINDS OF JOKES FOR ALL KINDS OF FOLKS

Joi̶r̶ e Page 1 of 2

are they Lo! RI ̶a̶t̶ ̶e̶ ̶l̶ Jo̶ ̶━━━━━
siamese   Josŝie Josephine
Twins?

.y. MI
You can e-mail us at ̶m̶ ̶━━

- Clerical work involving medical terminology
- Advanced word processing
- Advanced spreadsheet work
- Office automation macro programming
- Light drafting with AutoCAD™
- Laboratory work

- Clerical work involving engineering/manufacturing terminology
- PC hardware and software upgrades
- Data entry
- Relational database work
- Light AutoLISP programming

We are both experienced and qualified in all the above occupations. We are especially effective as a team. We prefer a predictable (and reasonably student-compatible) work schedule, but don't prefer any shift over another. We are very flexible about most other employment-related issues. We are currently available (together or individually) to work in the greater Detroit area.

Lori's long term goal is to be involved in any way, hopefully significant, in computational biochemistry. Like Josie, she plans to spend the next few years preparing for application to and success in graduate school.

Josie's long term (approx. 5 years) goal is to get accepted into a graduate program in and later (approx. 9 years) practice (in order of preference) osteopathic medicine, veterinary medicine, allopathic medicine or physical therapy.

Lori's qualifications

BS in mathematics from the University of Michigan.

Fluent in French. Literate in Russian and Spanish.

Completed C/UNIX (CIS 190), data structures (CIS 281) and database theory (CIS 283) at Oakland Community College.

Completed intro. to artificial intelligence (CSE 416), operating systems (CSE 450), mathematical statistics II (STA 428, not designed for non math/stats majors) and Engineering Graphics (ME 208) at Oakland University.

Josie's qualifications

Highly proficient with medical terminology.

Solid understanding of most office automation software products in widespread use today, especially the Microsoft™ Office™ suite.

Completed general biology I & II (BIO 153), human anatomy & physiology I & II (BIO 163-164), botany & zoology (BIO 154;&155), microbiology (BIO 261) and Phlebotomy (MDA 125) at Oakland Community College.

Completed Engineering Graphics (ME 208) at Oakland University.

There's always that one worker that helps themselves to a little something extra for free. This woman was very creative in defending her sticky finger actions.

Ex-treasurer of Episcopals gets 5 years

Church money stolen

SANTA MONICA
Ellen F. Cook
Thurs. 7-11-96

By Jeffrey Gold
THE ASSOCIATED PRESS

NEWARK, N.J. — The former treasurer of the Episcopal Church was sentenced to five years in prison Wednesday despite her claim she could not even remember embezzling $2.2 million.

"I condemn this crime and the greed that caused it," U.S. District Judge Maryanne Trump Barry told Ellen Cooke, 52, of McLean, Va.

Cooke claimed she suffered from a psychological disorder that caused her to steal and forget what happened later.

She spent much of the money on private schools for her children, remodeling of her Montclair home and a Virginia farmhouse, and air fare between the two residences.

She also charged the church $40,000 for jewelry, $30,000 in restaurant bills and thousands more in gifts from Steuben glass and Tiffany's.

"This defendant deliberately and meticulously, with knowledge then and now, looted the national church over a period of years for one reason and one reason only: to live the life of someone she was not," Barry said.

Cooke pleaded guilty in January to embezzling $1.5 million while working at the church's headquarters in New York from 1986 until her firing in 1995. A later audit discovered that $2.2 million was missing.

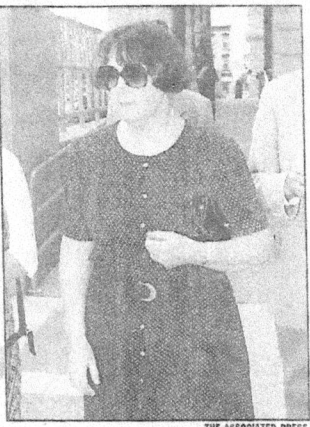

THE ASSOCIATED PRESS
Ellen F. Cooke, ex-treasurer of the national Episcopal Church, says she can't recall the theft.

In arguing for leniency, Cooke's lawyer, Plato Cacheris, said she suffered from "haughty, high-flying and reckless hypomania."

Cacheris said Cooke cracked under the stress of a miscarriage, a failed in-vitro fertilization, a mother who underwent brain surgery and a father who was diagnosed with terminal cancer.

Men & Women are Funny

How come when you meet the right person you know immediately but when you meet the wrong person it takes ten years of marriage to find out.

I'm single…yippy! Actually, I'm not so sure why I'm happy about it. I'm beginning to think that my headstone will read, "Here lies Kelly…still sleeping alone."

My friends say that I'm pretty and smart…which is why, of course, they are my friends.

You know you've been single too long when Valentines Day comes rolling along and you find yourself in the pet food isle searching for heart-shaped treats for your pet.

My marriage vows should have included the phrase, till debt do us part.

I should have known the marriage wasn't going to last when my man proposed, he asked me to take his last name…and add it to my checking account.

I want my husband to take me into his arms and whisper those three little words we all want to hear: You were right.

For the 10th wedding anniversary the traditional gift is tin, for us it should have been gold bars.

"A few years ago I lost 250 lbs."
Wow! How did that work?
"I divorced my husband."

My ex finally saw a doctor after we divorced. They discovered he had multiple personalities, one was a thief, one was a liar, one was mean and one was a lazy son of a gun.

I know the divorce wasn't all his fault; it takes two to make a marriage succeed or fail. When we went to see a marriage counselor, the counselor asked me if it was difficult to please my husband. I thought for awhile and replied, "I don't know, I never tried."

I don't understand women who marry murders in prison. You will notice most of them marry the murderer that has no chance for parole. I can just see their faces if they were to receive a call from the Warden.
Ring, ring
"Hello, Mrs. Murderer. This is Warden Joe. We have great news, the laws for life imprisonment have been

overturned and your husband, Charlie, has been released."

CLICK!

"Hello, Mrs. Murderer? Hello?"

Oh, Mrs. Murderer is packing her bags and getting ready to hop in her beat up Ford Pinto and high-tail it to Canada or Maine, whichever comes first.

A young woman came home while on college break. She told her mom, "Mom, I've got a case of VD." Her mother replied, "Put it in the fridge, your dad will drink anything."

I think I'm getting desperate for the touch of a man. Last week I stole an expensive item just so two big burly guys would tackle me as I left the store.

Love is blind, that's why we feel around so much.

Well, Hell did freeze over...I've got a date this Saturday night.

Dating is tough. I thought this guy really liked me but you can never tell. What was I to think when he said, "I want you to have my babies" I said, "Oh, yeah, wow! Sure, sounds good to me." He said, "Great, I'll drop them off at eight this Saturday night."

Bathing suite season is upon us! Time to diet. I'm working on getting down to my original weight, six pounds, seven ounces.

I divorced my husband because he had a mistress, she was a long-necked, shapely bottle of beer.

I know my ex is getting nicer because everyone is starting to wave at him using all five fingers.

I thought I married a country singer/songwriter. What I married was the country song, lot's of crying, cheating, lying, thieving

If you want to attract a man, forget the strawberry or kiwi scented shampoo. Get some steak or bacon-scented shampoo and they'll follow you in droves.

My date was so cheap he brought over a seven-dollar bottle of champagne. Drinking seven-dollar champagne is like taking a bubble-bath with dish-soap

There ought to be more accurate names for deodorants. Why don't they have names like, *Pitt Stop, No Sweat*, or for the deodorant that's so effective you don't even know it's there, *Vice President*.

I don't know why a feminine product is named *Always*. Why name it that? As if once a month isn't bad enough who wants to buy a product called *Always*.

I might be getting too desperate with my dating habits. Last night I met this really compassionate man at the local bar. I thought he said, "I can see you are really upset and would like to talk." Actually, he said "Hi."

I looked my name up in one of those, what does your name mean books. For Kelly it read: Doomed to live eternally single, living paycheck to paycheck.

I used to think that when I got married I would write poems and love songs for my man. (Snort!) Five years into the marriage I managed to squeeze out this little ditty: Light up a cigarette, sit on the can, guzzle another beer, that's my man!

A bad marriage is like a comfy bed, easy to get into and hard to get out of.

Going through menopause is like being Fiona in the movie Shrek. One day you are a beautiful princess and then you go to sleep and wake up an ugly ogre.

There should be a boot camp where you can send your husband. They would learn things like:
- How to wring out a dishrag
- How to replace the lining in the trash can
- How to replace the empty roll of toilet paper
- Learn how to say those three important words, "You were right"
- Learn how to use silverware
- Instead I think the husband comes with his own little manual that instructs:
- Never say you are sorry
- Always have an excuse
- Change your voice to a witch when quoting what your wife says
- Make mean, ugly faces to scare your wife when you are angry
- Make boo-boo faces so she feels sorry for you
- And most importantly, don't give up the remote control

ALL KINDS OF JOKES FOR ALL KINDS OF FOLKS

It's true I was in an abusive relationship but on the plus side I was never bored, what with all the crying, screaming, yelling, running and mind games.

It can be trying sometimes to be a woman. It may feel like we never get a break. First we get the period and then we get the pause, menopause that is. It should be called mental-pause. You can't remember a thing. You act mental. You look mental.

I've thought about getting married again but there is just one problem with that concept; they move in with you.

While in college when trying to start a conversation with the opposite sex you would ask, "What's your sign?" Now that I'm older the first question out of the gate is, "Do you have a job?" Followed up with, "You're not living in your parents garage or basement, right?"

Google the symptoms for a head cold and you will see that for men it reads as a life-threatening, debilitating disease and for women it reads that she should take two aspirin and get on with her life.

My date last night was just a little too country for me, he drank juice from a pickle jar. It was a picked pigs feet jar. Who thought of pickling pigs feet? "Hey! Don't throw them thar pigs feet away! Let's put 'em in a jar along with some vinegar and spices and let them set a good long while and woo-wee I bet they'll be tasty."

Sometimes I think wedding vows should include the phrase, "From this day forward, anything you say, can and will be held against you."

For our anniversary, my husband and I would do what came naturally. I would go shopping and he would lay on the couch with the remote control.

My ex wasn't that big of a monster. In fact he had some interesting features, like he had different colored eyes…two of them were blue.

My spouse and I never experienced marital bliss, only marital blisters.

When I got married I thought he was my night in shining armor, instead he turned out to be me nightmare

Mary: I should have known our marriage wouldn't last. I was born in the USA and he came from the land down under.

Eunice: Australia?

Mary: No, Hell

Driver shoots car after it quits on him

By SUE McCLURE
Staff Writer

SPRING HILL — When his car died on him, the owner got mad and decided to finish it off, emptying an AK-47 into the car's body.

The sight of a man standing on Saturn Parkway just after 10 p.m. Saturday with an assault weapon leveled at his car, pumping round after round into the car's body, was so strange witnesses did double — no, triple takes.

"I understand he unloaded three 30-round clips into the vehicle," said Maury County Sheriff Enoch George.

"We got seven or eight calls about it," said Crystal Mills, a Maury County E-911 dispatcher.

"People were driving by on the parkway and couldn't believe this guy was shooting at his car."

When officers arrived on the scene, they found the bullet-riddled 1988 Oldsmobile vehicle with no one inside.

"The man told officers his car had quit on him and he got mad and decided to shoot it," Mills said. "He was arrested with no problem

Offensive Funny Stuff

Q: What kind of battery does the electric chair use?
A: A DieHard

A guy comes home ashen-faced and his wife looks up and says, "What did the doctor tell you?"

"He says I only got six hours to live," the guy says. "Listen," he goes on, "Let's make the most of our last little while together. We'll go out and have a wonderful dinner, just the two of us."

"Oh sure, easy for you to say," the wife replies. "You don't have to go to work in the morning."

A ventriloquist was driving in the country when he was attracted to a large farm. He asked for and was given a tour.

As he was shown through the barn, the ventriloquist thought he'd have some fun. He proceeded to make one of the horses talk.

The hired hand, wide-eyed with fear, rushed from the barn to the farmer. "Sam," he shouted, "those animals are talking! If that sheep says anything about me, it's a damned lie!"

Q: What do you call a pretty woman in Russia?
A: A foreigner

Q: What's an Irish seven-course dinner?
A: A six-pack and a potato

Q: Why do Mexicans eat beans for dinner?
A: So they can take bubble baths

Q: How can you tell Dolly Parton's kids in a crowd?
A: They're the ones with stretch marks on their mouths

Q: Why do so may black soldiers die in war?
A: Every time their leader yells, "Get down," they stand up and boogie

Q: How do the Indians on the reservation greet one another?

A: HI! How are you? HI! How are you? HI! How are you?

The Chinese are gaining ground in the auto manufacturing field. Autos from the Chinese manufacturer, Chengfeng, are gaining recognition as they are being introduced at all the Auto Shows. They recently unveiled their newest, most expensive, luxury, top-of-the-line vehicle; they named it the Cha-Ching!

The Chinese have a popular small vehicle called The Armor. If you go to China you will see a lot of chinks in the armor.

I hate it when my boobs itch, it's like trying to scratch jello.

Q: Why don't blind people parachute?
A: Because it would scare the shit out of their dog

Q: What do you call a gay dentist?
A: The tooth fairy

Teen: What up oldster?
Old Man: Not yo pants!

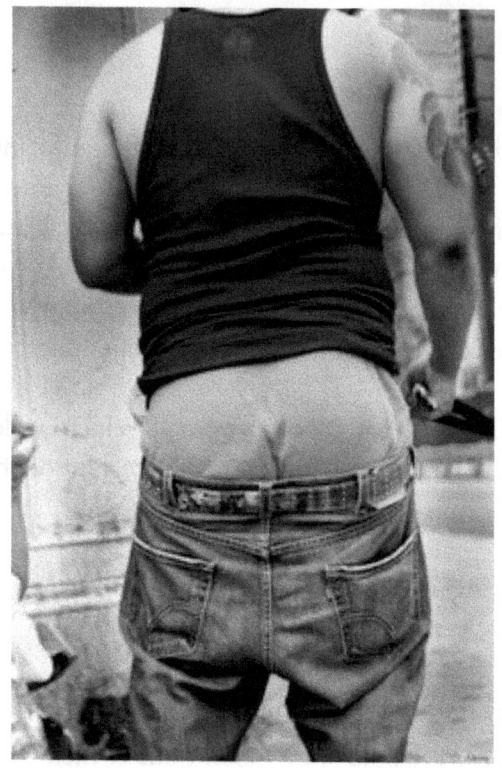

I hate the term co-dependent, it sounds like you are telling someone they are a co-asshole.

Q: What did the man name is new titty-bar
A: The Booby Trap

We made an impromptu visit to the beach the other day. I decided to relax and lay on the beach for a while. With no towel or chair available and having a rather large back-end I proceeded to use my hands to dig out a hole so I could comfortably half-lay, half-sit on the beach. I guess you could say I dug myself a new ass-hole.

They are coming up with a new Viagra-like drug for women, it's called Ho-Zac.

I don't trust psychics from the deep south. The last time I saw someone there, she rubbed her crystal ball and said, "I'm fixing to git a vision", she continued "Yer 'bout to lose a tooth."

Someone told me that I was anal-retentive, I replied "I couldn't agree with you more; I've been married to the same butt-head for eleven years."

Forget those stupid doggie sweaters and bandannas, let's get doggie underwear for some of the bigger brutes. I mean some of that junk hangs real low.

I've noticed that a lot of black families will name their children by combining the names of both the mother and father. Mom might be named Denise and dad is Kenneth, hence they name their little girl, Kenisha. Or mom is named Martha and dad is Keith so they name their son, Markeith. It's a good thing my white family didn't follow suite as my mom's name is Pat and dad is Joe, I could have been named Potato.

I recently attended a Green Bay Packers football game in Wisconsin. Wanting to fit in I purchased a great big foam hat shaped like a piece of cheese. I blended in as one of the cheddar-heads. Thankfully this team wasn't located in the outskirts of say, Oklahoma where manure is the main commodity, otherwise the fans would all be shit-heads.

Q: What did Michael Jackson do after selling his Neverland Ranch?
A: He bought Boys Town

Ever notice that it never feels the same when you try to massage yourself than when someone else does it. The same goes for picking your nose, it never feels the same when someone else tries to do it.

Two hunters are out in the woods when one of them collapses. He's not breathing and his eyes are glazed. The other guy whips out his cell phone and calls 911

"I think my friend is dead!" he yells. "What can I do?"

The operator says, "Calm down. First, let's make sure he's dead."

There's a silence, then a shot. Back on the phone, the guy says, "OK, now what?"

Getting Old is Funny

I don't know how to date all over again. I didn't do it right the first time around. Last time I dated older guys and married one, of course that didn't work out. This time I think I'm dating guys too young. I went to pick up my date the other day and he came running out... with tennis shoes that lit up.

Friends try to help me in the fashion department. One friend had the nerve to tell me I dressed better ten years ago, I don't know why they said that, I wear the same clothes.

A woman called the newspaper so she could report an obituary for her husband. She asked them to write, "Max is dead." The reporter asked her if she would like to have anything else written up to which she replied, "No, just write, Max is dead." The reporter let her know that obituaries have a six-word minimum. She thought for a bit then said, "OK, write, Max is dead, Toyota for sale."

Keeping in line with his Midwest straight-to-the-point lifestyle, his headstone read: Here lies John, he was hatch, matched and dispatched.

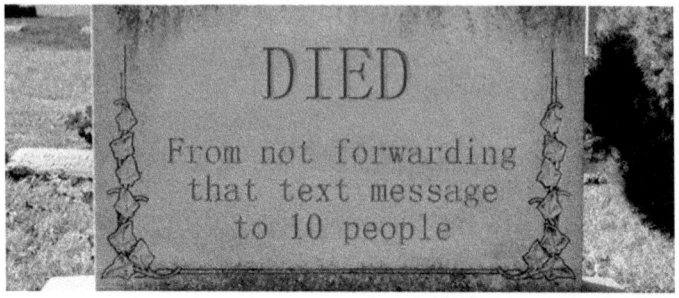

I remember when my attitude was, look all you want, just don't touch. Now, I'm like, touch all you want, just don't look.

You know you're getting old when you get up in the middle of the night to pee and it's only 10:00 p.m.

It's true that grey hair makes you look distinguished; it distinguishes you from the younger looking people.

It's too bad that when we age our hair turns that awful color grey. It would be so much more pleasant to say, "I'm going green around the temples." Or, "I've got a full head of cobalt blue hair."

Now that I've gone through menopause I sleep like a baby; I wake up and pee every two hours.

I think I've been doing stand-up comedy too long. The last time I was about to go on stage someone said to me, "Go out there and break a … hip."

A little friendly advice to all the young woman that want to marry an older man for his money. Just make sure he has a big house with a lot of stairs and different rooms, that way you can run from room to room up and down the stairs yelling, "Catch me if you can!"

Now that I've gone through menopause my gyno exam hurts like hell! I expect to look up and see the Dr. wearing a rubber suit and holding a whip.

Horoscopes and psychics always state the obvious. I went to see a psychic, she looked at my palm and announced, "I see you getting fatter and more tired in the future." Well, duh.

The older we get our lives feel like some great mystery that is unfolding. "Why do I have these weird red bumps on my forehead?" "What is going on with this funky patch of hair growing on my butt?" "Is that skin just growing from out of nowhere?"

Grandpa is turning 90. I made him a prune cake for his birthday because I wanted to give him something that would move him.

Our date got off to a bad start. Frustrated with my date, I told him that if he were my husband I'd poison his coffee. He quickly replied, "If you were my wife, I'd drink it."

Prayers tend to change as we get older. When I was younger I might have prayed, "I'm sorry God for calling my sister a poop face." Now that I'm older my prayer might be, "Thank you God for I was able to poop today."

Menopause is a lot like being Fiona in the movie *Shrek*. One day you are a pretty, slim, attractive young lady, then overnight you become a frumpy, plumpy, grumpy old woman.

Old Timey Story Jokes are Funny

A family of moles just woke up to a beautiful day on the farm. Papa mole went to the mole hole, he squeezed a bit and poked his head out of the hole and said, "I smell Farmer John's bacon and eggs cooking." Mamma mole went to the hole and squeezed and squeezed and finally she was able to get her head out of the hole too. Mamma said, "I smell pancakes!" Baby mole ran to the hole where he squeezed and squeezed. He twist and turned and tried to get his head out of that hole too. He finally gave one last big squeeze then finally had to give up where in dejection he said, "I smell mole-asses."

There was a table where three newlywed couples were enjoying their breakfast. With the first couple, the man said, "Pass me the sugar, honey." The second couple, the man says, "Pass me the syrup, sweetie." The third couple, the man says, "Pass me the bacon, pig."

A woman came into the police station to report her husband missing and described him as "29 years old, 6 feet 3 inches tall, blond and handsome." "I know your husband," said the desk sergeant. "He was bald, fat and forty." "I know, " the woman said, "but who wants HIM back?"

A woman was lying in bed dying. She asked her husband to lean down as she had a something important to tell him.

Woman: I'm dying Vern

Vern: I know baby

Woman: Vern, I have a confession to make before I leave you

Vern: What is it baby

Woman: I've been unfaithful to you ever since we first married

Vern: I know baby, that's why I poisoned you

A bad man was sent to Hell. Upon entering hell he was greeted and told he could choose between three places to spend eternity.

He was escorted to place number one where the door was opened. He peered in and saw that everyone in the room was standing on their heads. There was water everywhere, including all over the floor where they had to stand on their heads. In the corner of the room was a very large, intimidating creature that appeared to be watching over everyone. The man didn't think that option looked too appealing so he was escorted to the second room where the door was slowly opened to reveal that everyone in the room was standing on their heads, just like the last room. The difference was this room was filled with jello. The people had to shift as the jello was sloshing all around them. As before, there was a very large, mean looking creature standing in the corner. The man didn't think that room was very appealing and it looked like a very sticky, slippery way to spend eternity.

Finally, he was shown how he could spend eternity by peering into room number three. He noticed everyone was standing around chatting and drinking coffee. They were, however, standing in poop. The poop was up to their knees. The stench was awful. As he noticed from the other room viewings, there was also a tall, mean looking creator standing in the corner, apparently watching over everyone. He pondered his decision. With room number three he could get used to the smell, he further reasoned, he could at least socialize and have something to drink during eternity. The man said he selected room number three to spend eternity. He was tossed into room number three. He gagged and heaved but eventually he was able to get over dealing with the smell. He made his way to the coffee machine and poured himself a cup of coffee. Just as he was about to take his first sip, the creature in the corner yelled, "Times up, coffee break is over, stand on your heads!"

The woman greeted her husband at the door when he came home one evening after a long day at work. She put a blindfold on him and told him she had a surprise for his birthday. The man became excited thinking of all the wonderful things his wife may have for him for this his special day. She slowly walked him towards the dining room. Perhaps she prepared an elaborate, delicious meal for him he thought.

She told him that she was going to leave the room for a few minutes while she went to get something. He sat, alone in the room in the quite darkness and reflected on the day he had. Earlier in the day his co-workers had treated him to a birthday lunch at the local eatery. He had eaten a big bowl of franks and beans. By now the beans were really tearing up his stomach. He felt a rumbling in his stomach. He needed to pass some gas. He thought he better hurry up before his pretty wife returned with her surprise so he let out a big, loud fart. Oh it was a smelly one too. He quickly swiped at the air around him hoping to dissipate the smelly vapors. Oh no, he felt another one coming on, so once again he leaned to his side in the chair and let it escape. Whoo! This one was especially funky so he quickly waved his hands at the air around him. Surely she would be coming back soon so he decided to hurry up and squeeze another one out of him. This one was so loud he thought she might hear it from another room. With that last one he felt as though he had finally relieved himself of the gas that was brewing inside him. He could relax.

Feeling good about his ability to relieve himself during the time she was gone he was happy when she returned to the room. She walked over to where he was and started to take off his blindfold. "OK honey" she began, "are you ready?" She took off the mask and all his family and friends jumped up from around the table and yelled, "Surprise!"

A man had a heart attack. As he was leaving the hospital to go home to recuperate his doctor gave him some advice. "Remember," the doctor told the couple, "no physical exertion for your husband. He just had a major heart attack. And that includes sex. It could kill him." That night, to avoid temptation, the man slept downstairs on the couch. At three a.m., he woke up and started for the stairs. Halfway up, he met his wife. "I was just coming up the stairs to die." "And I," she replied, "was just coming down the stairs to kill you."

A woman placed an ad on a dating site where she wrote she was looking for a future husband. She requested just three things from him. One, he must not hit her. Two, he must not run away. Three, he must be great in bed. A few days later her doorbell rang. She opened the door and was greeted by a man that said the following: "I am here to answer your ad. As you can see I have no arms so I can not beat you. I have no legs so I can not run away." She replied, "Well, how are you in bed?" The man answered, "I rang the doorbell, didn't I."

A man and a beautiful woman went out on a first date. It was a starry night in Madrid, Spain, the air was crisp and the man was looking forward to impressing his young love with the special meal he had arranged at a well-known restaurant located at the top of the famous bullfighting arena. "You are going to love this delicious delicacy that is prepared for just three couples after the bullfight has ended." He exclaimed with great anticipation. "How wonderful" she said, "I heard that Top of El Toro is indeed the finest restaurant around. I didn't know they have a special meal set aside for just three couples. You must really love me to go out of your way to arrange for us to be the special couple that is served this special meal tonight. Thank you dear love." They went directly to the restaurant and sat at the special table reserved for the three lucky couples. Three chefs proudly arrived with their covered dishes. The first chef announced "Ole!" as he lifted the lid and set the dish before the first couple. It was two huge mounds smothered in delicious gravy. The second chef also announces loudly, "Ole!" as he lifts the lid and set the dish before the second couple. It was two huge mounds covered in hot, spicy salsa with lots of chips for dipping. Finally the third chef sets his dish in front of the couple on their first date and lifts the lid as he says, "Here you go." The dish contained two tiny mounds that sat atop some noodles and sauce." The man asked the chef, "Why did the other couples get a dish with two huge mounds of meat and we received this tiny portion?" The chef replied, "The bull won."

A very proper woman inherited a parrot, Penrod, from her father's estate. The problem was that Penrod used vulgar language. After several embarrassing experiences when she hosted her bridge club, the woman told her minister about the problem. The minister said his female parrot "is a saint. She sits on her perch and prays all day long. Bring your parrot over. She'll be a good influence on him." The woman took Penrod to the minister's house and when the cages were placed together, Penrod hopped through the open doors and said, "Hi baby! How about a little lovin'?" "Hallelujah!" sang the female parrot. "You're just what I've been praying for."

Funny Songs

I can't make fun of today's songs because my generation and generations before me had some pretty funky music they partied to. In the fifties they had Splish, Splash I was takin' a bath, a rub dub just relaxin' in the tub. Who can forget the one-eyed, one-horned flyin' purple people eater. I said Mr. Purple People Eater what's your line? He said "Eatin' purple people and it sure is fine" The 90's had a country song where the singer had one request "Prop me up beside the jukebox if I die. Fill my boots up with sand put a stiff drink in my hand." One of my favorite songs from the 70's was Timothy. Timothy, along with two other fellas found themselves trapped in a cave. Eventually dinnertime rolled around and there was nothing to eat. The two stronger guys started to look at the weaker Timothy. Next thing you know there are just two guys in the cave, leaning back with full bellies and licking their fingers. As soon as they were ready to doze off they were rescued from the cave and they began to sing, "Timothy, where on earth did you go? Timothy, God I loved you so." I bet.

Remember the name game? The name game was made popular in the 60's by singer, Shirley Ellis. She'd sing out, "Shirley, Shirley bo burly, banana, fanna, fo firley,

Shirley!" So I say, come on everybody let's rhyme a name: Obama! Obama, Obama, fee, fi, fo, yo mamma, Obama! That was fun.

Repeat after me: Ew! Ah! Ew, Ah! Ew, Ah, Mah! Ew, Ah Ma sunshine, my only sunshine. Ew make me happy when skies are grey.

The bear went over the mountain, the bear went over the mountain. The bear went over the mountain, to see what he could see. To see what he could see, to see what he could see. And what do you think he saw, and what do you think he saw? He saw a box of ex-lax, he saw a box of ex-lax. And what do you think he did? And what do you think he did, what do you think he did? He ate the box of ex-lax, he ate the box of ex-lax. He ate the box of ex-lax and what do you think he did? What do you think he did, what do you think he did? He made another mountain, he made another mountain, he made another mountain and that's the end of that!

Monkey Fun!

Her butt is lumpy, her face is chunky, but of course, she's a monkey

Swinging from the trees, swinging from the vines

Just having a good ol' monkey time!

Her arms and legs are long and hairy, her body smells oh so funky

But of course, she's a monkey

Swinging from the trees, swinging from the vines
Just having a good ol' monkey time!

Swinging from the trees, scrapping her knuckles and knees
She's a monkey, a monkey, aint it grand to be a monkey!

Kelly & Eddie

The Getting Old Song

You can die your hair
Clip your nose
Lower your pants and
Show your crack…BUT you're still gonna look your age

You can smoke a joint
Drink Martinis
Show your crack…BUT you're still gonna look your age

You can inject your lips, inject your boobs
Tummy-tuck and jazzercise
Show your crack…BUT you're still gonna look your age

Oh yeah, you're gonna die, I'm gonna die, we're all gonna die
Die, die, die, ding-dong dead
Die, die, expire
Terminate
Gone
Passed away
Dirt nap

It's hard to accept that our bodies change over time. We tend to think we are still the same as when we were at our peak, like maybe in our twenties. I go shopping for underwear and still buy the same size I bought twenty years ago. I go home, try on the underwear and find they are too tight and creeping up my butt. I wash the underwear and put it back in my drawer never to use them again because they are uncomfortable. I can't seem to throw them away as I have to admit my butt has ballooned to half the size of a Kardashian butt. It makes me have the blues to spend money on underwear I don't use. I've got the…

Underwear Blues

My rear end needs alignment
But I still buy the smaller ones
Ya see I buy 'em way too tight
So they hug my buns

I've got those
Frilly, lacey, short & long
But not a thong
Too tight underwear blues

Ya know my belly is a waist-land
Can you stomach what that means
I don't lose weight, I misplace it
So it must be in my jeans

I've got those stretch it to the max
Any shade you might choose
Too tight but it's no problem
I've got those too tight, creeping up my butt
Underwear Blues!

Unemployment Blues

Staying up till 2
Sleeping in till 10
Oprah's off the air
I'm bored and staring at the walls

I've got those
Wrinkled, shabby, forgot to shower
Countin' down the hours
Unemployment Blues

Sending out the resume
Into a black hole
Do those H.R. folks even have a soul? I've got those
Mmmmmm, I want a good paying, nice co-worker, great boss want the job blues

Stay Away Blues

Stay away, stay away, stay away!
I've got those *Stay Free, Always*, once a month blues

I'm kinda mean
I'm really bloated
To ease the pain
I need ten aspirin coated

Don't come near me, I'm not feeling well
I can't talk, I can only yell
So, Stay away, stay away, stay away
I've got those *Stay Free, Always*, once a month blues

The College Drinking Song

Drink to sister, Colleen, sister Colleen, sister Colleen
Drink to sister, Colleen, she's with us tonight
She's happy, she's corny, she's with us by golly
Drink to sister Colleen, she's with us tonight

Drink chug-a-lug! Drink chug-a-lug! Drink chug-a-lug!

The Men and Women Song

Men, men, men, men
Men, men, men, men

They stink, they fart, they sweat, they smell

Women, women, women
Women, women, women

They're moody, broody, snooty, they shout, they pout, they squeal

The Work Song

You've got to dodge it
You've go to duck it
You've got to finally throw your hands up and say, ffff-Friday, please hurry and come along.

The Breakup Song

I dated a musician for a couple years and finally he was fed up with me. Instead of telling me to my face that he was breaking up with me he invited me to his concert and dedicated this special song to me.

Hello Babe
This is your man and Honey
I'm here to tell you
You an' me are through
Yeah, you know it's true
You done me wrong
And now, I'm giving you the gong
How do you like this song?
No, it aint happy, it's blue
'cause honey, I'm through with you.

Song of Bitterness

Gonna fight these lousy blues
I'ts over between me and yous
Gotta get better, can't you see
Won't dwell on what you've done to me

You Son of a Bitch!
You Son of a Bitch!

You rotten, lousy bastard!
I'm not gonna dwell on what you've done to me

The Smith Song

I'm quite sure that nobody enjoys
Getting out of bed earlier than expected

I'm positive that no one wants to leave
The table before they are finished eating

I know it's not fun going out into the cold when
You are quite warm and comfortable where you are

All these things happened to me during the midnight hours
Of April 2nd, 1961
I was rudely awakened while sleeping in my built-in waterbed

Before I knew it, the waterbed had sprung a leak and I
Had fallen through the flesh-toned bed frame

I had a terrible headache because something was squeezing my head
I felt like a tube of toothpaste as my entire body was being squished

I thought there was a party going on as I heard pans clinking
Bright lights and people shouting
"It's a girl, Mrs. Smith, it's a girl"

Kelly Smith

Good heavens, I had just been born and to a family named Smith

Smith, Smith, Smith, Smith, Smith

Happy Birthday!

I was young and needed the money.

My Man Song

Light up a cigarette
Sit on the can
Guzzle another beer
That's my man!

Spider lips and grasshopper toes

Oh, spider lips and grasshopper toes
Are mighty good to eat
They're chewy & they're crunchy
Plus they're extra sweet!

Oh, spider lips and grasshopper toes
Are not so hard to find
They're in the store, down isle 4
Next to the frozen porcupines

My Body Went Over the Hill

My body went sagging southwards
My body is no longer a thrill
My body is slower than molasses
My body went over the hill

Oh, bring back, bring back
Bring back my body to me, to me
Bring back, bring back
Bring back my body to me

The Curious Husband

My husband went out to see the tornado
I went to the basement to flee
It made a great rustle and rumble
Oh bring back my husband to me

Oh, bring back, bring back
Bring back my husband to me, to me
Bring back, bring back
Bring back my husband to me

Funny Words & Sayings

Bugaboo - One of the industry big bugaboo's is the lack of education for skills needed

Brouhaha - There was such a brouhaha over his graduation

Conniption - Before you go into a conniption, here's a snack to tide you over before dinner

Chicanery - The number of judges disciplined has not gone up but the level of chicanery has soared

Don't make me no never mind

Don't make me poison your food

Goose Egg - My goodness, that is a big goose egg on your head

Harrumph

Highfalutin

Holy Flying Monkeys

He's bigly braggadocious

Hideous - He wore a hideous sweater

He made me dizzy as a witch

How are you?
Terrible!
Why?
I'm broke, busted, disgusted and can't be trusted

Hootenanny - What happens when the H1-B hootenanny comes to an end

Hell in a handbasket - You're all going to hell in a handbasket

Hoi-Polloi - The Hoi-Polloi can swim in their own private pool at the club

However kindly we peer at her portraits, she still looks like a Basset Hound in a bonnet

Her merriment and saucy back-chat quickly made her the prison pet

I don't give a rats ass

I hate myself for loving you

I'm circling the drain

It's just a little wife lie

I'd lie awake at night performing an autopsy on our relationship

Lickety-Split - I'll get your papers for you lickety-split

Mosey - Why don't you mosey on over here

Ostentatious - Their new garage was ostentatious for the neighborhood

Ripsnortin' humdinger

Snarky

Snafu

Screeching Halt - Their love affair came to a screeching halt

Sheeple - Look at the sheeple doing what he tells them to do

Someone throw a net over me and drag me in

Sniggering - The audience left the theater sniggering at the debacle called a play.

Skedaddle - She skedaddled out of town keeping one step ahead of the creditors

She summons a gang of foul fiends from hell

The jig is up

Well shut my mouth with sweet potato pie

You're a Jack-a-Ninny

You're a Nincompoop

You're a Shameless She-Devil

Yer just as pretty as a petunia in a patch of chigger weeds

God, He's Funny!

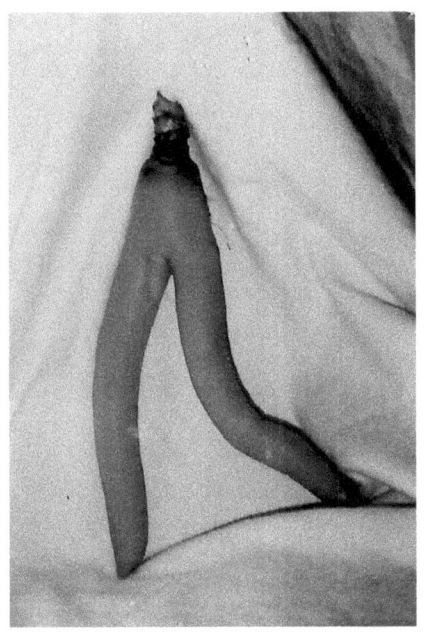

Proof that God has a sense of Humor

Q: What kind of pet does the religious family have?
A: A praying mantis

Q: What kind of socks does the religious person wear?
A: Holy ones

Q: What did the religious parents name their twin sons?
A: First and Second Thessalonians

Q: what time of day was Adam born?
A: Before Eve

Q: What is the difference between a Catholic and Pentecostal service?
A: One has a stand-up and sit-down service and the other has a jump-up and down service.

Did Jesus ever exclaim, "Oh my…self!"

Hell: A place where you are damned if you do and damned if you don't.

Child: Lord, what is a million dollars to you?
God: A penny.
Child: Lord, what is a million years to you?
God: A second.
Child: Can I have a penny?
God: Just a second.

Eddie Murphy's 'Donkey' in *Shrek,* had nothing on Balaam's feisty beast in Numbers 22. What did Balaam's donkey say to him the third time Balaam beat her for refusing to take her down a path where the angel of the Lord was waiting to kill Balaam?
A) Yeeeow! Now *that* hurt!

B) Now, I've had enough of that, you slaphappy, drunken fool!

C) What's with you? Haven't I been a decent, God fearing donkey? Have I acted this

odd before; don't you think that means something is wrong with where you want me to go?

D) Whip me one more time and you'll get the ride of you life!

Answer: C

Luke 8:26 -33 details Jesus casting demons out of a young man and sending them into a nearby heard of swine. Does this story have you craving...

A) Deviled Ham

B) Pickled pigs feet

C) Bacon

D) all of the above

Answer: D

What are we meant to learn from Matthew 7:3 when Jesus says, "And why worry about a speck in your friend's eye when you have a log in your own?"

A) The Lord was using humor to make a point

B) They really had specks and logs in their eyes back then

C) Here comes a fresh slice of humble-pie served by the Lord

D) Hop off your high-horse

Answer: D

Genesis 2:18 'The Lord God said, "It is not good for the man to be alone. I will make a helper suitable for him." Afterwards did Adam exclaim…

A) "Awesome, a match made in heaven!"

B) "This is now bone of my bones, and flesh of my flesh; she shall be called woman, for she was taken out of man."

C) "Hey, you took one of my ribs!"

D) "Can she cook?"

Answer: B

Adam was newly created and Eve was just formed when the following is stated in Genesis 2:25 'Now although the man and his wife were both naked, neither of them was embarrassed or ashamed.' Do you think…

A) Well, I guess not. Freshly minted by God. I'd strut my stuff through the garden just as proud as the peacock that Adam just named.

B) Give them a few decades, they'll be jumping behind the bushes and reaching for the fig leaves for cover.

C) A and B but not D

D) That's because they are sinless at this point

Answer: D

Which of these is a name from the Bible:

A) Skeeter

B) Jethro

C) Billy-Bob

D) Bubba

Answer: B Jethro was the father-in-law to Moses

What was the profession of Amos:

A) Priest

B) Potter

C) Carpenter

D) Shepherd

E) Famous cookie maker

Answer: D

What was the ninth plague in Egypt:

A) Frogs

B) Darkness

C) Pimples

D) Excessive hair growth

E) Water turning into blood

F) Locusts

Answer: B

After Jesus applied mud to the blind man eyes, where did he tell him to go to wash it off:

A) Jordan river

B) Pool of Siloam

C) Dead Sea

D) Sea of Galilee

E) Bathroom sink

F) Garden hose

G) Niagara Falls

Answer: B

In Isaiah 3:17 there were some women acting high & mighty, better-than-thou. This highfalutin attitude upset the Lord so He punished the women by making them bald. Talk about knowing how to hit a woman where it hurts! I can just imagine God saying to them, "And if you keep it up I'll throw you into instant menopause, where you will gain 30 pounds and nothing, I mean *nothing* will get it off."

Genesis, chapter five, lists how long everyone lived. Chapter five starts off with Adam living to be 130 years old, he fathered Seth who lived to be 930 years old, Enosh lived to be 905, Jared died at 962, on and on to the grand-daddy of them all, Methuselah who lived to be 969 years old. The very first verse in chapter 6 begins, "Now a population explosion took place upon the earth." Well, I would guess so, no one was dying!

In Luke 8:32 -33 Jesus cast the demons out of a boy and into a nearby heard of swine. The pigs become crazed and immediately they rush over a cliff and fall into a lake below where they drowned. This is the first time we had Sooey-cide.

Also in Luke, chapter 19 verse 40 Jesus said "If they keep quiet, the stones along the road will burst into cheers!" This is the first mention of a rock concert.

Here we see the first UFO in 2 Kings 2:11 "As they were walking along and talking together, suddenly a chariot of fire and horses of fire appeared and separated the two of them, and Elijah went up to heaven in a whirlwind."

1 Kings 17:4 shows us where fast-food delivery originated: "Drink from the brook and eat what the ravens bring you, for I have commanded them to feed you." I wonder what they brought...figs, leaves, seeds, burgers & fries, who knows.

In the book of Deuteronomy it states that Moses gave three long sermons and then died. Three long sermons can kill anyone

A favorite hymn I like to sing after a long sermon is Free at last, free at last, thank God almighty I'm free at last!

The pastor announced, "In honor of us worshipping on April 15th, tax-day, let us open our hymnal to hymn number 1040: *I Surrender All*

Some church songs have you singing the same refrain over and over. 'I love the Lord, I love the Lord, I love the Lord, I love the Lord, I love the Lord...woo-wee I think I've fallen into a trance."

Mary & Joseph lose Jesus in Luke chapter 2. I can not begin to imagine what that panic attack felt like! For three entire days he was missing. I can hear everyone yelling and calling out his name. "Jesus! Where are you? Jesus! Jesus Christ! You better come home right now or so help me you'll be sorry!" On the second day they probably had a scary conversation with God, "Hello God. It's true, we've lost your only son. We could use a little divine help right about now."

Today we have security guards to watch over our money at the bank but back in Biblical times they had Eunuch's. The Eunuch were those that guarded the Queen's treasury (see Acts 8:26). To prevent the Eunuch from being tempted for sex and then have someone steal the money, they had to be castrated. And we think a drug screen and background check is a strict requirement for getting a job.

Near the end of the Old Testament in the book of Zephaniah, Chapter 3, verse 17 it says that God loves us so much He will sing a happy song about us. I wonder what kind of song he will sing for me. Will it be "Welcome to my world, won't you come on in." or "Hello Kelly! Well, hello Kelly! It's so nice to have you back where you belong." Perhaps a more realistic song will be like, "Oh my darling Kelly, you were born, laughed, loved, succeeded, failed, tried, and now you've died. See my arms are open, run and jump, I'll catch you and toss you high. You're the apple of my eye."

My husband and I pray together. His name is John and for dramatic effect after I finish saying my portion of the prayers I say, "and now God, heeeeeeres Johnny!"

Christians: We don't gossip; we have prayer chains
Christians: We don't gamble; we have bingo
Christians: We don't get high; we have coffee

Christians are harder on each other than they are with non-believers. A Christian to a non-believer will say something like, "Oh, poor sinner, God loves you." But heaven-forbid a Christian says or does something wrong. Their fellow Christian will cut them down to size with a remark like, "How could you! You said 'poop' and you call yourself a Christian!"

Farts are evidence that God has a sense of humor.

In the book of John, chapter 14, verse 2 God says he will prepare a room for us in His mansion. I wonder if it will be like the show Extreme Home Makeover or any of those other home make over shows where they reveal the new home by moving a bus or a big sign. Will we die, go to heaven and after orientation walk by this glorious mansion where we are told to wait. Standing with great anticipation as God tells the angels to "Move that Cloud!" We run into our room just as happy as clams as we explore all the goodies God has put inside the room. "Hey, there's my Mark Spitz poster and look, my own garden with a gazebo!" Or for the burly man there's a fire pit and shooting range nearby.

Prayers tend to change as we get older. When I was younger, I might come before the Lord and pray, "Forgive me Lord, for I had sex." Now that I'm older I might come before the Lord and pray, "Thank you Lord, for I had sex!"

I think there was a misprint in the Bible when it said in Ecclesiastes that the meek shall inherit the earth. I think it should have said the Geek shall inherit the earth. Just look at all the great geeks of our time, there's Bill Gates, Ross Perot, and RIP, Apple founder, Steve Jobs.

In 2 Kings, chapter 18, it mentions that men sat around eating dung. Perhaps this scene was mistaken with men sitting around eating Baby Ruth candy bars or giant Tootsie Rolls.

In the book of John, chapter 11, Jesus went to see Martha and Mary to raise their brother, Lazarus, from the dead. Jesus called in a loud voice, "Lazarus, come out!" The dead man came out, his hands and fee wrapped with strips of linen, and a cloth around his face. I can hear the shrieks of joy as those who had gathered were amazed and thrilled to have Lazarus return to live once again with them. I can also

Just hear the shrieks of terror from those that had a hard time taking in the vision of someone that was dead for four days, now coming out of a cave wrapped in strips of cloth, looking for all the world like a mummy. I can hear Lazarus try to talk beneath all the cloth, "Mmmmmble rrr thank you mmmmrhm cloth off please, mmmmrgh." At which point I'm sure that is when Jesus said to them, "Take off the grave clothes and let him go." Wee! What a cool miracle.

All Kinds of Jokes for All Kinds of Folks

www.ingramcontent.com/pod-product-compliance
Lightning Source LLC
Chambersburg PA
CBHW071740040426
42446CB00012B/2411